My Christian Year

Cath Senker

PowerKiDS
press.

New York

Published in 2008 by The Rosen Publishing Group, Inc.
29 East 21st Street, New York, NY 10010

First Edition

Picture Acknowledgments:
Art Directors and Trip Photo Library 4 (B. Turner), 8, 22, 23 (H. Rogers); Britstock Cover
(Tsuyoshi Kishimoto), 10 (Hinata Haga), 12 (Hideo Haga), 14 (Tsuyoshi Kishimoto), 21 (Takashi
Yoshida); Circa Photo Library 16, 25 (John Frye), 26, 27; Eye Ubiquitous Title page, 9, 11 (Bennett
Dean), 18 (Mike Kipling), 19 (L. Fordyce), 24 (Mike Alkins); Hodder Wayland Picture Library 7
(Penny Davies), 15 (Zak Waters), 17 (Stuart Weir); Impact 20 (Christophe Bluntzer); Nutshell Media 5
(Yiorgos Nikiteas), 13 (Sue Cunningham); World Religions 6 (Christine Osborne).

Cover photograph: Dressed up for carnival in Trinidad and Tobago.
Title page: A harvest festival procession in Barbados.

Library of Congress Cataloging-in-Publication Data

Senker, Cath.
  My Christian year / Cath Senker. -- 1st ed.
     p. cm. -- (A year of religious festivals)
  Includes bibliographical references and index.
  ISBN-13: 978-1-4042-3729-2 (library binding)
  ISBN-10: 1-4042-3729-1 (library binding)
  1. Church year--Juvenile literature. 2. Fasts and feasts--Juvenile literature. I. Title.
  BV30.S46 2007
  266--dc22
                                    2006028000

Acknowledgments: The author would like to thank Janay, June and Colin Bromley, and Morgan
O'Flaherty, Head of St Mary Magdalen School, for all their help in the preparation of this book.

Manufactured in China

Contents

A Christian life

Christians believe there is one God. He made the world and looks after it. God loves every living creature.

Christians believe that Jesus is the Son of God. They follow Jesus' teachings in their holy book, the Bible. Christians feel that God's power is always with them. It is called the Holy Spirit.

Christians worship in churches. This girl has lit some candles in a church in Greece.

4

This is Janay. She has written a diary about the Christian festivals.

Janay's diary

Wednesday, November 12

My name's Janay Bromley. I'm 9 years old. I've got a brother named Mitchell and a sister, Ciara. We have a hamster named Pumpkin. I love swimming and going shopping. At home, I like reading and playing with my sister and my friends. We're members of the Catholic Church.

There are many Christian festivals. Most festivals celebrate events in Jesus' life, especially his birth and death.

The Christian symbol is the cross.

Sundays

Every Sunday

Sunday is the Christian holy day. It is a day of rest. People like to spend the day with their family and church friends.

At church, the priest or minister gives a sermon. He or she reads from the Bible. People pray and sing hymns or other songs.

These Christians are singing and dancing in church to worship God.

Many children go to Sunday school to learn about being a Christian.

Some Christians worship quietly. Others prefer loud, joyful church services.

Janay's diary
Sunday, November 23

We went to church this morning. Our church is run by Father Foley. He is nice and he always helps people. Today, I was an altar girl. I like being part of the church community. On Sundays, we read the Bible. We always have a family lunch. I like Sundays, because I get to spend lots of time with my family.

Advent

November 30–December 24

Advent is the start of the Christian year. Christians prepare for Christmas by thinking about how they could become better people.

Advent calendars and candles help to count down the days until Christmas Day.

This girl is lighting the first candle on an Advent ring.

One door on an Advent calendar is opened every day until Christmas.

Monday, December 8

Today was the ninth day of Advent. I opened another door of my Advent calendar. I'm really excited about Christmas —only 16 more days to go! Yesterday at church, the priest lit the second Advent candle. He wore a special robe and talked about the birth of Jesus. At school today, we rehearsed for the school play. I'm going to sing carols with the choir, too.

Some churches have an Advent ring. It has four colored candles and one big white candle. On the first Sunday of Advent, one colored candle is lit. Every Sunday, one more is lit until all four are alight. The white candle is lit on Christmas Day.

Christmas

December 24–January 6

At Christmas, Christians celebrate the birth of Jesus. He was born in Bethlehem, in the land of the Jews.

Most people celebrate Christmas on December 25. Orthodox Churches hold the festival on January 6. Many churches hold a service on Christmas Eve. It is called Midnight Mass.

A Christmas parade in Perth, Australia. In Australia, Christmas comes in the summer. Many people celebrate outdoors.

A nativity scene in Goa, India. Christians believe that Jesus was born in a stable in Bethlehem.

Christmas Day is a holiday in many countries. People go to church and sing carols. At home, they give presents and have a special meal.

Janay's diary

Thursday, December 25

Last night, on Christmas Eve, we read the Christmas story. We hung up our stockings and said our prayers. This morning we woke up early—it's Christmas Day and I was too excited to sleep! We gave our baby Jesus doll a kiss and put him in his toy crib. Then we opened our presents. After Mass, we had Christmas lunch. I always think of Jesus on Christmas Day. Without Him, we would not have Christmas.

Epiphany

January 6

Epiphany celebrates the story of the Wise Men. They came to see baby Jesus, bringing three special gifts.

Epiphany means "to make known" in Greek. Christians are happy that Jesus was made known to many people.

Children dressed up as the Wise Men, in Austria. The Wise Men brought gifts of gold, frankincense, and myrrh.

Spanish children in a procession to celebrate the Wise Men's visit to baby Jesus.

But the Jewish leader King Herod was not happy. He thought that Jesus might try to take his throne. So he told his soldiers to kill all Jewish baby boys. Luckily, Jesus escaped with his parents, Mary and Joseph.

Janay's diary
Tuesday, January 6

Today, it was Epiphany. We went to Mass with Grandma, Grandpa, Auntie Jackie, and my cousins. Some children from the church acted out the story of the Wise Men. The Wise Men followed a special star, which led them to baby Jesus. The story shows how important Jesus was, because the Wise Men traveled for a long time to find him.

Shrove Tuesday

February

Shrove Tuesday is the day before Lent.
Some Christians go to confession.
They tell their priest about any bad
things they have done and pray to God
to forgive them.

**Young dancers at
a Lent carnival in
Trinidad and Tobago.**

This boy is making pancakes on Shrove Tuesday.

Shrove Tuesday is sometimes called Pancake Day. In New Orleans and France, it is also called Mardi Gras (which means Fat Tuesday). People make pancakes. In the past, this was to use up fatty foods before Lent. In some countries, there is a carnival.

Janay's diary
Wednesday, February 25

Yesterday, it was Shrove Tuesday. Daddy made pancakes from flour, eggs, and milk. We ate them with maple syrup—they were yummy! We decided what to give up for Lent. My whole family gave up something. I decided to give up candy. Giving up something for Lent helps us to be thankful for what we have every day.

Lent

March/April

Lent lasts for 40 days before Easter. Christians think about things they have done wrong. They believe that if they are sorry, God will forgive them.

On Ash Wednesday, the priest marks a cross of ash on people's foreheads.

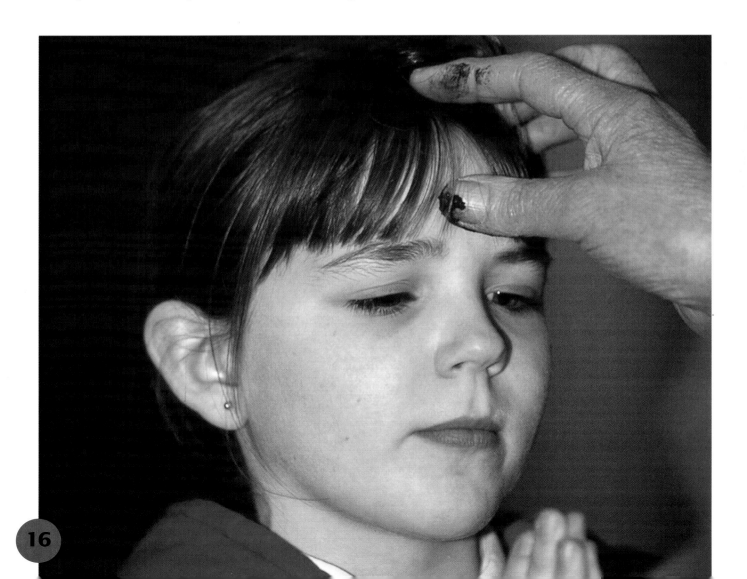

At Lent, Christians try to give up a food they enjoy, such as chocolate. It reminds them that Jesus spent 40 days in the desert without food.

In Britain, Mother's Day is during Lent. People say prayers for their mothers and give them a present.

This girl has given her mother some flowers for Mother's Day.

Janay's diary
Sunday, March 28

Today, it was Mother's Day. We made breakfast in bed for Mom to show how much we love her. Then we went to church. Afterward, we took Mom out for lunch. I haven't eaten any candy for over a month because it's Lent. There are still another 13 days to go. It's been really hard giving up candy, but it's worth it. Mom says it's good for my teeth, too.

Holy Week

March/April

The last week of Lent is Holy Week. It is the most important Christian festival. People celebrate the last week of Jesus' life.

On Palm Sunday, they remember how Jesus rode into Jerusalem on a donkey. Many churches hold processions and people carry crosses made out of palm leaves.

A Palm Sunday procession in Spain, with a statue of Jesus.

Christians around the world remember Jesus dying on the cross. This ceremony is in the Philippines.

On Maundy Thursday, Christians think about the Last Supper that Jesus had with his friends. Then on Good Friday, they remember how Jesus died on the cross.

Janay's diary
Friday, April 9

Today, it was Good Friday. In England, we have hot cross buns—we ate them today hot with melted butter—delicious! The buns have crosses on the top to remind us that Jesus died on the cross. This week at school, we learned all about how Jesus died. We heard how his friends were very sad. It was a very busy week at school learning about things.

Easter Sunday

March/April

On Easter Sunday, Christians remember Jesus' Resurrection. It is a joyful day.

After dying on the cross, Christians believe that Jesus rose from the dead. This was a wonderful miracle. It showed that life could win over death.

On Easter Sunday, churches are decorated with spring flowers. The church bells ring out.

People light candles and lamps. The candles and lamps stand for new life.

These Greek Christians are at Mass on the night before Easter Sunday.

20

Janay's diary
Sunday, April 11
Today was Easter Sunday. I wanted to open my Easter basket, but we had to wait until after church. It was nice to celebrate Jesus rising from the dead, because he is so special. Easter eggs stand for new life. We give them to remember how Jesus was given new life after he died. When we got back from church, we gave Easter eggs to each other and had a big family meal.

An Easter parade in Miami. Some people wear decorated eggs.

Ascension and Pentecost

May/June

Forty days after Easter, Christians celebrate Ascension Day. They believe that 40 days after his Resurrection, Jesus ascended (rose) to heaven to be with God.

Ten days after Ascension Day is Pentecost. Christians remember the coming of the Holy Spirit. This is God's power working in the world.

A banner showing the coming of the Holy Spirit surrounded by Jesus' followers.

At Pentecost, new members are welcomed to the Christian Church. This boy is at a special ceremony called confirmation.

The Holy Spirit helped Jesus' followers to spread his teachings. This was the beginning of the Christian Church. Pentecost is the Church's birthday.

Janay's diary
Friday, May 21

Yesterday, it was Ascension Day. At school, we learned about Jesus' ascension to heaven. It was very important, because it helped people to believe what Jesus taught. We thought about Jesus going up to heaven. Then we had to paint what we thought it was like. I drew a big flash of light rising up to the sky.

Harvest festival

September/October

Harvest festival is in the fall.
It celebrates all the foods and
flowers that grow in the earth.

Christians thank God for these good
things. They decorate their church
with fruit, vegetables, and flowers.

**A harvest festival
procession in Barbados.**

These children have brought bread and corn dollies to church for the harvest festival.

Janay's diary
Wednesday, September 22

Today, it was the harvest festival. We brought lots of food into school for people who needed it. There was a harvest display at Mass. We gave thanks to God for giving us rain and sun to help the harvest. The priest talked a lot about the needy. Afterward, I went with the Brownies to the old people's home. We brought food and helped to make lunch.

Christians like to share food with people who are not as lucky as they are. Often they take presents of food to people in need. They collect goods to send to people in poor countries.

25

All Saints' Day

November 1

On All Saints' Day, Christians remember all their saints. Saints are people who lived a good life. They followed Christian ways and helped other people.

Some saints were killed because they were Christians. For their good deeds, the Church made them saints.

Some saints have their own day, when people remember them. On All Saints' Day, Christians honor the saints who don't have their own special day. People sing hymns about them in church.

A picture of Saint George, the saint who protects England. His saint's day is April 23.

Saint Francis of Assisi, the saint who protects animals and cares for nature. His saint's day is October 4.

Janay's diary

Monday, November 1

Today was All Saints' Day. It's a very special day. We remembered all the people who have done good things for others. At school, we talked a lot about all the saints. I hope that one day Mother Teresa will be a saint. She helped lots of sick and poor people. All Saints' Day is also special, because it's my birthday!

Christian calendar

November 30–December 24

Advent
Christians prepare for Christmas.

December 25

Christmas
People celebrate the birth of Jesus.

January 6

Epiphany
This festival celebrates the Wise Men visiting baby Jesus.

February

Shrove Tuesday
The last day before Lent.

February/March/April

Lent
Christians remember the 40 days that Jesus spent in the desert without food.

Ash Wednesday
The shape of a cross is marked on people's foreheads with ash.

March/April

Holy Week
Christians remember the last week of Jesus' life.

Easter Sunday
People remember Jesus rising from the dead.

May/June

Ascension Day
People remember the day that Jesus rose up to heaven.

Pentecost
This is the birthday of the Church.

September/October (in Northern Hemisphere)

Harvest festival
People thank God for giving us food from the earth.

November 1

All Saints' Day
Christians celebrate their saints.

Glossary

Advent A time of preparation for four weeks before Christmas. Advent means "coming."

altar girl (or boy) A child who helps the priest in church.

Bible The Christian holy book.

carnival A big festival, with music and dancing in the streets.

Catholic Church The Roman Catholic Church is led by the Pope, or Holy Father.

Church The whole community of Christians. A church is also a building where Christians meet.

community The people who live in the local area. Here it means the Christians living in the area.

confession Telling the priest about any bad things you have done.

Father Another name for priest.

holy Connected with God.

Holy Spirit The power of God in the world today. The Holy Spirit helps people to do what God wants.

honor To show that you admire and respect someone.

hymns Religious songs that Christians sing together in church.

Last Supper The last meal that Jesus ate with his followers.

Lent The season of 40 days before Easter.

mass A service that uses bread and wine to help people remember Jesus.

minister In some churches, the minister is the person in charge.

Mother's Day It is celebrated on the second Sunday in May in the United States and the fourth Sunday of Lent in Britain.

nativity The birth of Jesus Christ.

Orthodox Churches Churches such as the Russian and Greek Church. They are sometimes called the Eastern Churches.

palm A straight tree with no branches and lots of long leaves at the top.

priest The person in charge of a Catholic church.

Resurrection Jesus' rising from the dead.

sermon A talk about a religious topic.

services Religious ceremonies in church.

For Further Reading

Books to Read

Christianity (Religions of the World) by David Self
(World Almanac Library, 2006)

Christianity (World Religions) by Alan Brown (Walrus Books, 2005)

Easter (Rookie Read-About Holidays) by David F Marx (Children's Press, 2001)

The Kid's Book of World Religions by Jennifer Glossip
(Kids Can Press, 2003)

What You Will See Inside A Catholic Church by Michael Keane (Skylight Paths Publishing, 2002)

World Religions (History Detectives) by Simon Adams (Southwater, 2004)

Places to Visit

Los Angeles County Museum of Art

5905 Wilshire Boulevard

Los Angeles, CA 90036

Tel: 323-857-6000

www.lacma.org

Metropolitan Museum of Art

1000 Fifth Avenue at 82nd Street

New York, NY 10028-0198

Tel: 212-535-7710

www.metmuseum.org

Due to the changing nature of Internet links, Powerkids Press has developed an online list of Web sites related to the subject of this book. This site is updated regularly. Please use this link to access the list:
www.powerkidslinks.com/ayrf/christian

The author

Cath Senker is an experienced writer and editor of children's information books.

Index

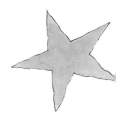